AMAZING
MIGRATIONS

HARRIET BRUNDLE

©2018
Book Life
King's Lynn
Norfolk PE30 4LS

ISBN: 978-1-78637-223-9

All rights reserved
Printed in Malaysia

Written by:
Harriet Brundle

Edited by:
Kirsty Holmes

Designed by:
Gareth Liddington

A catalogue record for this book
is available from the British Library.

AMAZING MIGRATIONS

CONTENTS

WHAT IS A HABITAT?

The place where an animal lives is called its habitat. A good habitat has food, water and a safe place for an animal to raise their **young**.

Although these animals are all birds, they live in very different habitats.

Desert

There are many types of habitat and each one is different.

Animals live in habitats that meet their needs. Some habitats meet the needs of lots of different animals, so there will be many **species** living there.

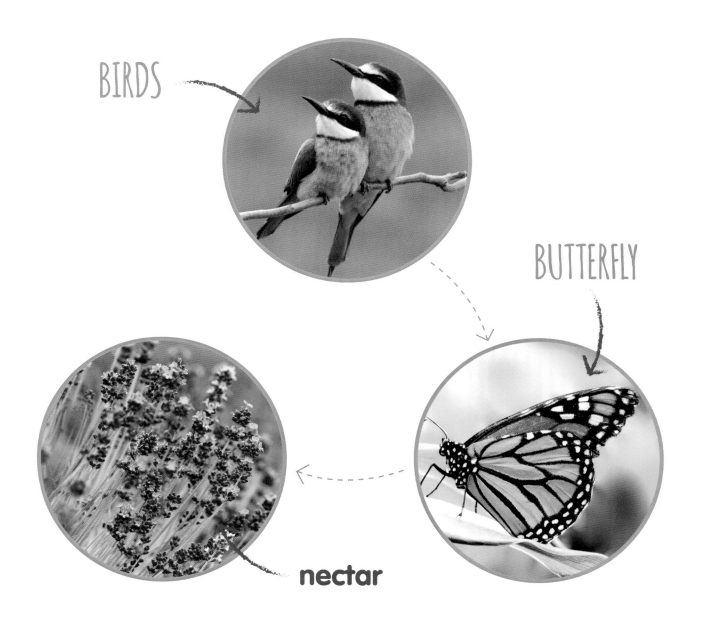

BIRDS

BUTTERFLY

nectar

Some habitats might have plants that animals can use for food or shelter. Some animals eat other animals in their habitat to **survive**. This is called a food chain.

WHAT DOES MIGRATION MEAN?

Migration is the movement of animals from one place to another. Some animals move small distances when they migrate. Others travel hundreds of kilometres.

These geese are heading south for the winter.

When birds migrate, they often fly in a 'V' shape. This lowers the amount of wind **resistance**. This means the birds use less energy and can fly farther.

Animals often migrate to find better **living conditions**. During the winter months, some species of bird fly south to warmer places where they can find more food.

Animals also migrate to **breeding grounds** so that they can go on to lay eggs or have their young.

Birds and insects lay eggs from which their young hatch.

ARCTIC TERNS

The Arctic tern is known for having one of the longest migrations in the world. The birds travel almost 80,000 kilometres in total.

Arctic tern

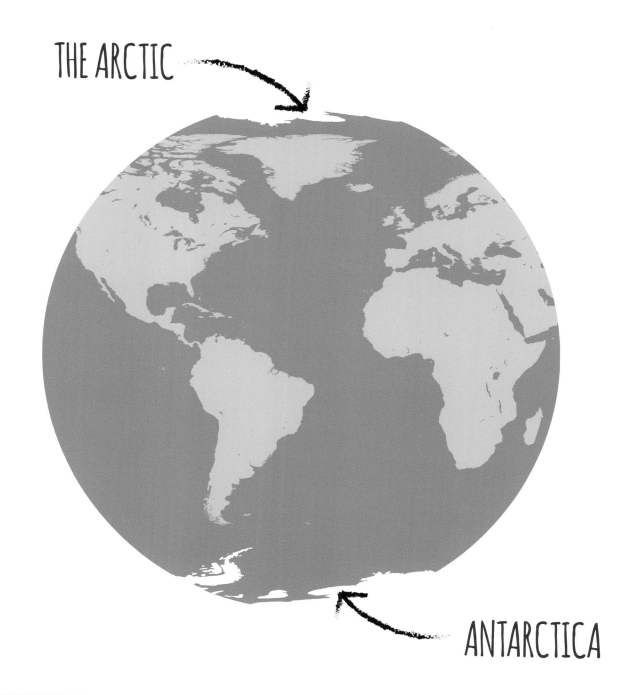

THE ARCTIC

ANTARCTICA

The birds travel all the way from the Arctic to Antarctica and back again. The main reason for their migration is to reach breeding grounds.

MONARCH BUTTERFLIES

Monarch butterflies travel over 4,000 kilometres on their journey. The butterflies leave the U.S.A. and Canada to move away from the cold weather.

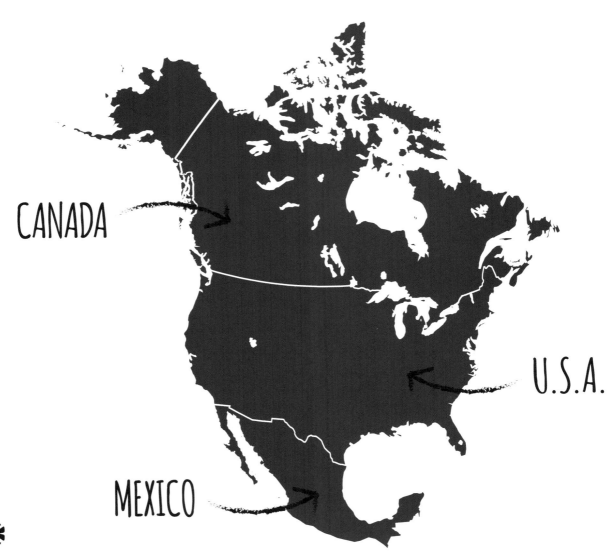

CANADA

U.S.A.

MEXICO

Thousands of butterflies migrate at the same time!

The butterflies migrate to Mexico where the weather is warmer. In Mexico, they find a **mate** and lay their eggs.

SEMIPALMATED SANDPIPERS

The semipalmated sandpiper is a small bird that migrates during autumn and spring each year. As many as 300,000 birds travel together when they make their journey.

The birds eat lots of food before they make their journey to give them plenty of energy.

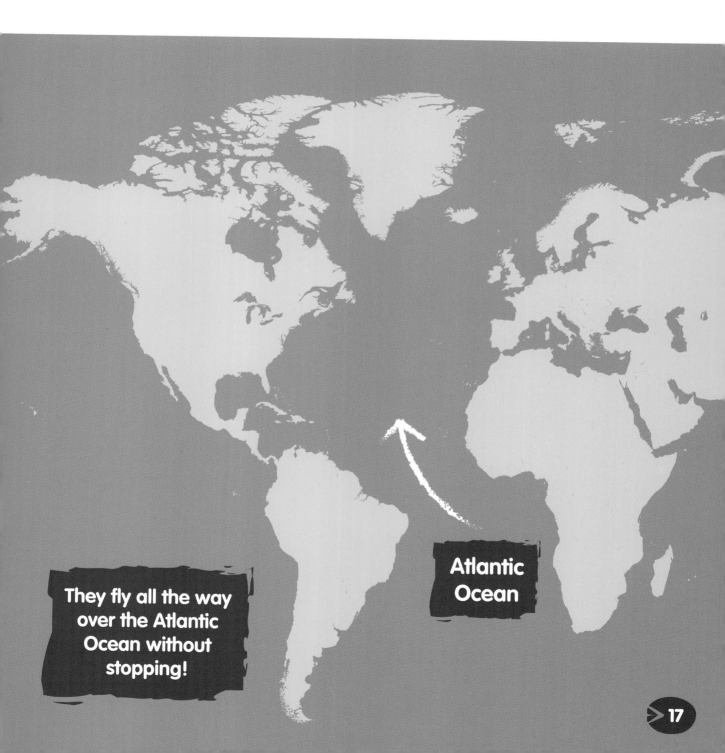

Atlantic Ocean

They fly all the way over the Atlantic Ocean without stopping!

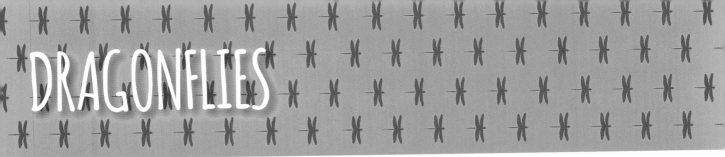

DRAGONFLIES

Dragonflies have the longest migration of any insect on Earth. They travel over 17,000 kilometres when they migrate.

A Dragonfly

Birds often eat the dragonflies as they migrate.

The dragonflies use their wings to glide through the air. This helps them to save energy and fly farther.

The Earth is becoming hotter over time because of something known as climate change. Climate change is causing **weather patterns** to change.

Birds and insects use the **temperature** of the air to tell them when to start their journey. Climate change makes the air warmer, so they start their journeys at the wrong time.

1. The names of these birds have been jumbled up. Can you work out which is which?

Swallow   **Goose**   **Arctic Tern**

2. Think of a bird or insect you have seen at the park, in your garden, on television or even at the zoo. Can you draw it? Do you know what it's called?

3. What might you expect to see in your animal's habitat? Does it live in the trees? Or in the grass? Add this to your drawing!

GLOSSARY

breeding grounds — an area where birds, fish, or other animals go to breed

living conditions — the things that affect that way something lives

mate — a partner (of the same species) who an animal chooses to produce young with

nectar — a sugary liquid that is found in flowers which is eaten by insects and other animals

resistance — a force moving against something else

species — a group of very similar animals or plants that are able to produce young together

survive — continue to live

temperature — how hot a person, place or object is

weather patterns — weather that we have become used to happening at particular times

young — an animal's offspring

INDEX